Musical Instruments

Xylophone

By Nick Rebman

level
1
little blue
renders

www.littlebluehousebooks.com

Little Blue House is distributed by North Star Editions:
sales@northstareditions.com | 888-417-0195

Produced for Little Blue House by Red Line Editorial.

Photographs ©: Shutterstock Images, cover, 7, 10–11, 15, 17, 19, 23, 24 (top left), 24 (top right); iStockphoto, 4, 9, 13, 21, 24 (bottom left), 24 (bottom right)

Library of Congress Control Number: 2022911116

ISBN
978-1-64619-705-7 (hardcover)
978-1-64619-737-8 (paperback)
978-1-64619-798-9 (ebook pdf)
978-1-64619-769-9 (hosted ebook)

Printed in the United States of America
Mankato, MN
012023

About the Author

Nick Rebman is a writer and editor who lives in Minnesota. He enjoys reading, walking his dog, and playing rock songs on his drum set.

Table of Contents

Playing the Xylophone 5

Glossary 24

Index 24

Playing the Xylophone

I play the xylophone.

It makes a nice sound.

The xylophone has many bars.
The bars are made of wood.

I hold two mallets in my hands.
I use the mallets to hit the bars.

mallet

The large bars make
low notes.
The small bars make
high notes.

My teacher shows me
how to play.
She tells me which bars
to hit.

I learn how to read sheet music.

I start playing slowly.

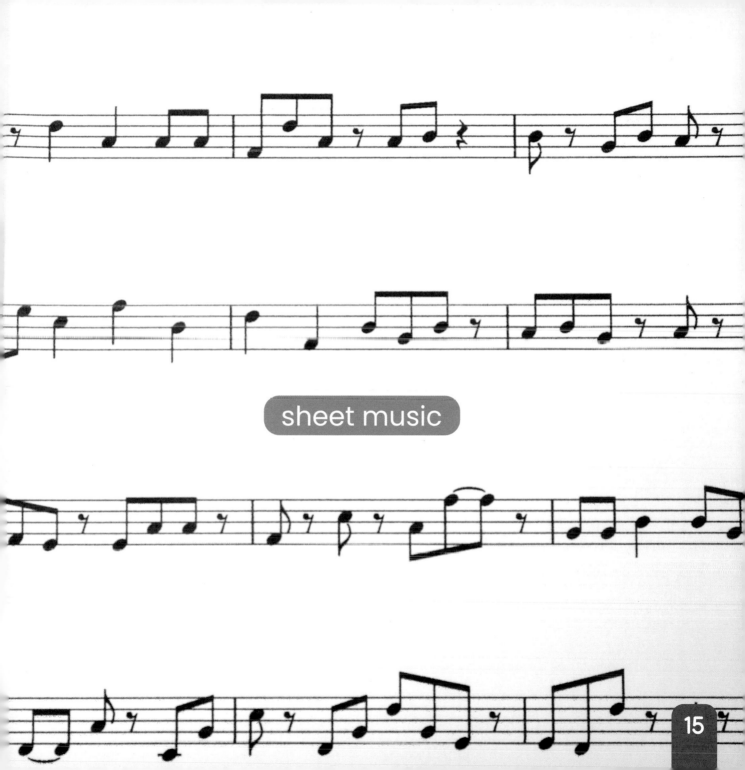

I practice every day.

I get better and better.

Soon I can play faster.

17

I learn many different songs. I play them again and again.

I like to play with my friends. Sometimes we play outside.

Other people watch us.

They enjoy our songs.

I love playing

the xylophone.

Glossary

bars

sheet music

mallets

teacher

Index

N

notes, 10

P

practice, 16

S

sheet music, 14

T

teacher, 12